CAMPBELL-EWALD
Reference Center

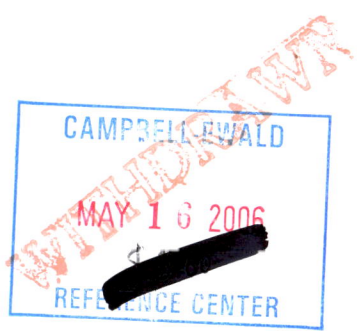

watching words

Ivan Chermayeff and Tom Geismar

move

Chronicle Books   San Francisco

About *watching words
mo v   e*

In the early years of the twentieth century, both writers and artists began to break down the distinction between words and visual forms, using the actual typographic elements of text to create powerful images. Apollinaire's words rained down the page; Marinetti's virtually exploded on the page. A.A. Milne filled his 1926 *Winnie the Pooh* with phrases that bounced and jumped with his characters. And by the early fifties, Saul Steinberg was giving simple words and letters a life and character of their own: Never before had "No" been stated so graphically.

As young graphic designers in the late 1950s, we were attracted to these artistic devices because we recognized the potential power of combining words and images into a single visual expression. In a search for the most direct forms of communication, we were equally attracted to some of the highly expressive elements found in the homemade, sometimes crude street signs of the city—the way that amateur sign makers used juxtaposition or other small manipulations so that the letters formed not only words but also familiar images.

In 1959, along with our colleague Robert Brownjohn, we decided to explore the evocative potential of words by compiling a handmade experimental notebook composed of pasted-up letters and words, all in one size of one typeface, Standard Bold. The proofs we cut up were all made from hand-set metal display type, the only method available at that time.

What we had in mind when putting together *watching words move* was to more vividly express the actual meaning of words, using only small changes in spacing or positioning or substituting of characters. This was done without bringing anything else to the table—no changes in type size, no variations in boldness, no use of color or contrast.

Our love of letters also included a love of their kindred characters: punctuation, symbols, shorthand, and abbreviations. And while we're at it, we thought, why not mix the "language" of numbers with the language of words? Can't they come together to speak just as plainly, or perhaps even more forcefully?

In 1962, the resulting notebook which we titled *watching words move*, was printed, in reduced size—the original was $8\frac{1}{2}$ by 7 inches and included as a forty-eight-page insert in the influential British magazine *Typographica*. At the time, the booklet caused considerable stir within the fledgling graphic design community. Today its ideas have become part of the standard graphic design curriculum, and in movie titles, television commercials, and print advertising, one can still see the influence of that little insert from over forty years ago.

In *watching words move*, we looked at the words and did to them what they themselves suggested.
The notebook was a demonstration of how the designer, using only the simplest means, can make certain words more evocative, and expressive of feelings, thoughts, and suggestions. In other words, words can have personality, and they don't need special typefaces or funny hats to do so.

Ivan Chermayeff
Tom Geismar

ha
lf

st len

o

no thing

över   lb.ound   "nch

'oot SHrINK ca$h

aboutface

clown

nO!se   exi   t

addding

subtrcting

multimultiplying

div id ing

nippea

tyxpewriter

TElephone

dea♎

advertisiNg

2uo

3rio

4tet

togetherness

tophalf

blo⊥⊥o

inflation

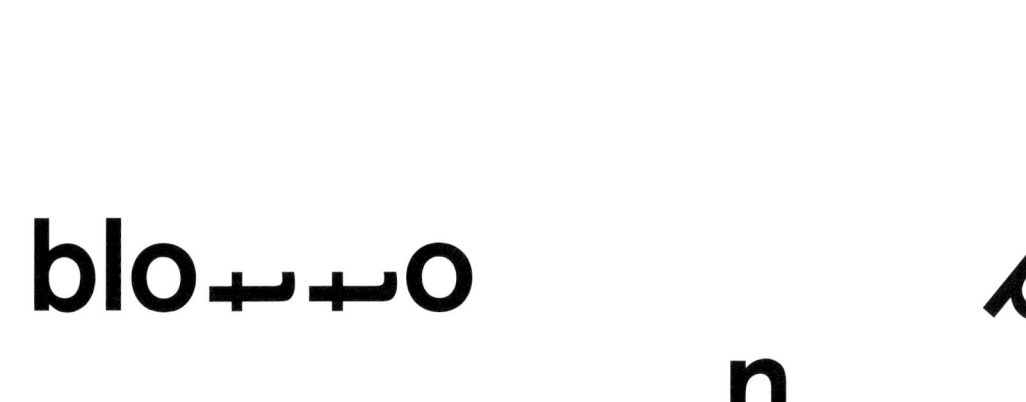

s∠c⊏oana__∠s._s

elesoapvisbeerion

missiles   aut₀m

unemplyment ooo

biles

zip

¢ents

MIR

qer

sawww

ROR

ero	
1ne	6ix
2wo	7even
3hree	8ight
4our	9ine
5ive	10en

rreeppeeaatt

ag&in&ndag&in

qu"o"te

=qual

blOated

falling
,

av

ditto

oid

EXPEN$IVE

r e g

e¢onomical

imented

NON-CONFORMISt

temperature

hot°

thimk backward

spe-cif´i-cal-ly

f_oor

per.od

com,ma

c:l:n

mamMoth

+dd

−tract

xultiply

div÷de

f1rst

hang

confused

o

ballo n

/eaning   upside

имор

ᄋ

clim

breaking cutting

splitting bending

fallin

g

s-s-t-u-t-t-e-r

sexxx

TΩNNEL

surpr!se

incomplet

s ec re t

agreeem nt

?uestion

!xclamation

s   t op!

end

Thoughts on *watching words move*

Michael Carabetta is creative director of Chronicle Books.

Steven Heller is art director of the *New York Times Book Review* and co-chair of MFA Department of the School of Visual Arts.

Kit Hinrichs is a partner in Pentagram.

George Lois is a designer and author of *The Art of Advertising* and *What's the Big Idea?*

April Greiman is founder and principal, Made in Space, Los Angeles.

■ For me, it all began with *watching words move*.

As a high school student in the sixties, I was interested in fine art and in commercial art, which we now call graphic design. I came across an article (I no longer remember where) on *watching words move*, and I sent a handwritten letter to Messrs. Brownjohn, Chermayeff, and Geismar to request a copy. When I received that slim black-and-white booklet, the proverbial lightbulb went off. I wanted to learn how to do what that book did: use the letters of the alphabet for something beyond forming mere words. *watching words move* literally moved me to pursue design.
I spent many study hall periods in the library poring over old *Graphis* annuals to learn who was who and who did what.

Back then, the idea that several decades and a computer revolution later I might not only be in a position to talk with the authors as my design peers, but also to extol this book's importance to my colleagues, and in turn the world, would have seemed a dream. To have had a hand in ensuring that this book—still encapsulating the essence of typographic design in the fully digital age—has a second life, with a new sphere of influence, is truly a dream come true.

Michael Carabetta

■ A verbal pun, we all know, is a comic play on words that have the same sounds but multiple meanings. Owing to the consequent strain required to issue a laugh, the pun is often considered an abominable form of linguistic humor (hence this rebuke: "two-thirds of a pun is pu"). A typographic pun is the substitution of an equivalent image for a letter or letters that visually define the word or words set in type. Commonly found in logotypes and trademarks where more than one idea is conveyed in a single graphic composition, it is one of the more prized design conceits.

Making type speak (so to speak) is as natural to designers as oxygen is to air-breathing mammals (of which most designers are a subspecies). Yet it was not until I found a battered copy of *watching words move* in the late sixties that I truly appreciated how type could be so keenly translated into visual language. The book was a breath of fresh air, and it radically changed the way I looked at, and ultimately designed with, type. Before encountering *watching words move*, I would specify inelegant novelty faces such as 'Ice' (snowcapped gothics), 'Log Cabin' (letters made from twigs), 'Lariat' (letters made from rope), or 'Chop Suey' (letters made from bamboo) when I needed to illustrate stories about cold, cabins, cowboys, or Chinese cuisine. All that changed the minute I saw the o's as wheels in "automobiles," the extra dot over the i in "ditto," and the upside down U in "TUNNEL" in this booklet. Although this clever display of type-play was not the first of its kind—during the teens, Italian Futurists injected sound into type through onomatopoeic poetics—the work of Brownjohn, Chermayeff & Geismar was a revelation when it was first published, and it has been the model for the possibilities in modern typography ever since.

Steven Heller

■ In 2004, I was fortunate enough to attend Chermayeff & Geismar Inc.'s fortieth anniversary party and exhibition at New York City's Cooper Union. What seemed like thousands of fans, groupies, and aficionados were guided between galleries by a series of "word/images" that entertained, informed, amused, and bewitched all who attended. These inventive images were taken from the publication *watching words move*, first created by Robert Brownjohn, Ivan Chermayeff, and Tom Geismar in the 1960s. I arrived in New York City at the same time, fresh out of the Art Center College of Design, so that booklet and other seminal works of Chermayeff and Geismar made strong impressions on me. As I look back over the intervening years, I find again and again those influences intertwined in my own work.

The staggering body of work created by this unique design group is copious and wide ranging, but their true genius is still epitomized by the imaginative word/imagery found in *watching words move*. No one can coax more meaning from the written word than Tom and Ivan. I find I am always looking for the emotional value within a specific typographic style, but in their hands, the power of each word is simply illustrated, not by using a fashionable typeface, but through a true understanding of language, and of how to expand its meaning through design.

Kit Hinrichs

■ The fifties and sixties were the golden age of Modernism in American graphic design. Paul Rand showed the way with the groundbreaking visual and typographic power expressed in his book *Thoughts on Design*, published in 1947, a visionary look at the emerging role of the contemporary designer. Among the first beneficiaries of his oeuvre were four other sensational New York talents: Bill Golden of CBS Television, Lou Dorfsman of CBS Radio, Gene Federico, and the inimitable Herb Lubalin. (Lubalin became the pivotal figure of typographic expressionism in America with his consummate talent for arranging, nestling, and elegantly fitting together classic letterforms in groupings that became almost sculptural on the printed pages.) God knows, as one of the youngest practitioners of the new graphic power, I designed many ads and promotion pieces in the fifties influenced by all their styles. As I did, I cast an admiring eye on the intelligence and witticisms of Robert Brownjohn, Ivan Chermayeff, and Tom Geismar. In 1959, during those exciting days when a new generation of conceptually minded talent was emerging, Brownjohn, Chermayeff & Geismar created *watching words move*, a publication of typographic sleight-of-hand and conceptual thinking unequaled in the ensuing forty-six years. In this tour de force, each word (impressively, every one set in the same typeface and size) is rendered to visually evoke its true meaning. *watching words move* is a marvel of powerful graphic statements, and is to this day a compelling tool for stirring the creative imagination.

George Lois

■ **In the beginning was *watching words move*...**

Well, perhaps this is a slight exaggeration, but, what the hell. It's hard not to give Ivan and Tom credit for the genesis of many a great typographic expedition, for much of the smartest design for the last fifty years (sigh…).

Let's face it—
only the really witty make us !claim
only the really intelligent make us ?uestion
only the really talented make the words not only move but   s   i
                                                               n
                                                                         g   !

April Greiman   w

Text copyright © 1959 by
Ivan Chermayeff and Tom Geismar.

Introduction copyright © 2006 Ivan Chermayeff
and Tom Geismar.

Essay copyright © 2006 by Michael Carabetta.
Essay copyright © 2006 by Steven Heller.
Essay copyright © 2006 by Kit Hinrichs.
Essay copyright © 2006 by George Lois.
Essay copyright © 2006 by April Greiman.

All rights reserved. No part of this book may
be reproduced in any form without written
permission from the publisher.

Library of Congress Cataloging-in-Publication
Data available.

ISBN 0-8118-5214-8
Manufactured in China.

Book and cover designed by
Chermayeff & Geismar Studio

Distributed in Canada by Raincoast Books
9050 Shaughnessy Street
Vancouver, British Columbia V6P 6E5

10 9 8 7 6 5 4 3 2 1

Chronicle Books LLC
85 Second Street
San Francisco, California 94105
www.chroniclebooks.com